CW00865530

For Jenny, Rosie and George.

BLOOMSBURY CHILDREN'S BOOKS
Bloomsbury Publishing Plc
50 Bedford Square, London, WC1B 3DP, UK
29 Earlsfort Terrace, Dublin 2, Ireland

BLOOMSBURY, BLOOMSBURY CHILDREN'S BOOKS and the Diana logo are trademarks of Bloomsbury Publishing Plc

First published in Great Britain 2022 by Bloomsbury Publishing Plc

Text and illustrations copyright © Matt Robertson, 2022

Matt Robertson has asserted his right under the Copyright, Designs and Patents Act, 1988, to be identified as Author and Illustrator of this work

All rights reserved.
No part of this publication may be reproduced or transmitted in any form or by any means, electronic or mechanical, including photocopying, recording, or any information storage or retrieval system, without prior permission in writing from the publishers

A catalogue record for this book is available from the British Library

ISBN: HB: 978-1-5266-3961-5; PB: 978-1-5266-3962-2; eBook: 978-1-5266-4981-2
2 4 6 8 10 9 7 5 3 1

Printed and bound in China by Leo Paper Products, Heshan, Guangdong

To find out more about our authors and books visit www.bloomsbury.com and sign up for our newsletters

Do you
LOVE
EXPLORING?

Matt Robertson

BLOOMSBURY
CHILDREN'S BOOKS

LONDON OXFORD NEW YORK NEW DELHI SYDNEY

G'day!

Hello!

Do you love exploring?

FROM THE TALLEST MOUNTAINS ...

... to the deepest oceans, animals all over the world have adapted to survive on every corner of the Earth. Discover **snakes** as long as **buses**, fish that are 400 years old and **sea** creatures that look like **poo**. New animals are being discovered every day. What will **YOU** find on your ...

WILD ANIMAL ADVENTURE!

Happy exploring

Hooowl!

Hello Amy

Are you ready to ...

- Join giraffes in the GRASS on a Savannah safari
- Meander up a MOUNTAIN with a Himalayan marmot
- Say Hi! to orangutans roaming through the RAINFOREST
- Sail the stormy seas to reach Volcano ISLAND
- Watch out for wolves and wombats in the WOODS
- Go wild in the ARCTIC with a walrus
- Dodge Thorny devils in the DESERT
- Outsmart an octopus in the OCEAN
- Find out which animal barks in the DARK
- Gasp and gawp at the WEIRDEST creatures in the world
- Discover the animals that need your HELP

Let's go!

Grasslands

RHINOS, ZEBRAS AND GIRAFFES ...

... these are just three of the grass-gobbling grazers you will find here. Grasslands can be found all over the world and are habitats where little rain falls but grass can still grow. One of the world's most famous grasslands is the African Savannah. Some of the most amazing grass-eating animals on Earth live here. But where there are grazers, there are always hunters ...

So look out for lurking lions!

THE AFRICAN SAVANNAH

1. From November to March, heavy rains flood the dry ground so there is plenty of grass and leaves to eat.

I'll explore this page from in here thanks!

AFRICAN ELEPHANTS

They are the largest land animals on Earth and eat for 16 hours a day.

6. Rain returns and THE CYCLE OF LIFE starts again.

I'm outta here!

GIRAFFES

The tallest mammals on Earth.

ZEBRAS

Scientists are still unsure why zebras have stripes.

5. The dry season forces animals away.

2. Animal poo fertilises the ground and provides food for bugs such as dung beetles.

BLACK RHINO

Don't spook a rhino! When they feel threatened, they usually charge at whatever has spooked them.

DUNG BEETLES

Dung beetles are the strongest animals on Earth.

GAZELLES

Live in super large herds.

3. Predators go hunting and eat their prey.

LIONS

Female lions (lionesses) do most of the hunting for their families.

HYENAS

They sometimes hunt in packs to take down larger animals.

4. Scavengers such as hyenas eat the scraps, stopping diseases from spreading.

Grasslands are GREAT!

OTHER GRASSLAND ANIMALS

Kangaroos of the Australian Savannah

These bouncy marsupials are related to koalas and wombats.

Bison of the North American Prairie

These are the largest land animals of North America.

The Giant anteater of the South American Pampas

They can swallow up to 35,000 ants and termites each day.

Mountains

NEVER PLAY HIDE AND SEEK WITH A SNOW LEOPARD!

Even at the top of the world you'll see animals of all shapes and sizes. Animals all over the planet are meandering up the sides of mountains or hiding in the highest forests. But they can be hard to spot thanks to their brilliant camouflage.

So Keep your eyes open wide!

ALPACA
The ancient Inca people raised alpacas for their quality wool.

Blue sheep are tasty to eat!

LOOK UP!
You may just spot ... the magnificent Golden eagle feasting on foxes, rodents, rabbits and hares.

Blue sheep

SNOW LEOPARD
These big cats have thick, spotty fur that keeps them well camouflaged, and wide feet for walking in soft snow. They are one of the only big cats that can't ROOOAR!

Shh, Blue sheep aren't actually blue.

BROWN BEAR

In Alaska, USA, Brown 'Grizzly' bears spend their time hunting for salmon by using long sharp claws to pin them down.

These bears can eat for up to 20 hours a day!

GIANT PANDA

Bamboo-eating pandas live high in the mountains of South-west China. They eat for up to 12 hours a day.

I love bamboo

MOUNTAIN GORILLAS

These powerful apes live in East-central Africa way up in high forests. Primatologist, conservationist and explorer Dian Fossey spent her whole life studying gorillas. And it's thanks to her that we now know so much about them - THANK YOU DIAN.

Thank you!

HIMALAYAN MARMOT

These mountain marmots make their homes three metres deep to hide from hungry predators.

Rainforests

DARK, WET and a little bit BITEY!

Rainforests can be found all over the world. In Africa, Asia, Australia, Central America and South America. They are homes to many different animals from the tiny **Pygmy marmoset** in the Amazon rainforest to the huge **African forest elephant** in the Congo rainforest. And guess what? Wildlife explorers are STILL finding hundreds of new species every year.

So WATCH OUT for some truly awesome animals!

Hyacinth macaw

Toucan

Scarlet macaw

THE RAINFOREST CANOPY

High above the ground, made up of dense layers of leaves, is the rainforest canopy. It is home to lots of monkeys and apes.

MONKEYS

Spider monkeys look a bit like spiders when they hang upside down.

Marmosets live in groups of eight to ten.

LA LA LA

Howler monkey
The howl of the loudest land animal in the world can be heard over three miles away.

APES

Gibbons communicate with each other by singing.

HOWL

KEEP THE NOISE DOWN!

GREEN ANACONDA

The world's biggest snake can grow as LONG as a bus! WOAH!

POISON DART FROG

These tiny blue jumpers are one of the most poisonous animals on Earth.

HUMMINGBIRD

The world's smallest bird is named after the sound its super-fast wings make.

Conservationists are working hard to stop rainforests from being cut down.

So respect our rainforests!

Goliath bird-eating spider

Orangutans
Their name means PERSON OF THE FOREST.

There can be up to 5,000 creatures living in a single tree!

HELLO!

Can you find these animals camouflaging (hiding) from predators?

Leaf-mimicking praying mantis

Chameleon

Giant leaf-tailed gecko

Jaguar

THE RAINFOREST FLOOR

The forest floor is a dark place where not much grows.

Ferns

Except for these!

Ginger

Moss

DARWIN

WOLF

PINTA

Whale shark

ISABELA

WOLF VOLCANO

Islands

AHOY THERE! ISLAND AHEAD!

Big ... small ... long and even heart-shaped, thousands of islands are scattered all over the world, each with their own ecosystems*. Keep your eyes open for the unexpected ...

Galapagos penguins

DARWIN VOLCANO

Welcome to the Galapagos Islands!

*An ecosystem means all the living things in one habitat.

This is the life

ALCEDO VOLCANO

FERNANDINA

GIANT TORTOISE

The oldest of these tough tortoises ever recorded was 152 years old!

SANTIAGO

Blue-footed boobies

SIERRA NEGRA VOLCANO

Hey, don't bite me!

RABIDA

CERRO AZUL VOLCANO

LAVA LIZARDS

These incredible lizards can grow back their tail (if it gets bitten off).

PINZÓN

THE GALAPAGOS ISLANDS!

These exciting islands are located in the Pacific Ocean near the west coast of South America. There are 13 major islands and 6 smaller islands and they're all formed by old piles of lava. Get ready to explore some of the most amazing animals on Earth!

Manta ray

GALAPAGOS FUR SEAL

Female seals can dive for up to 17 hours, mostly at night.

MARCHENA

GENOVESA

You can't catch me!

WAVED ALBATROSS

The largest bird in the islands.

N
W   E
S

AS DEAD AS A DODO

This flightless bird was so strange looking that some people thought it was a mythical creature. It became extinct hundreds of years ago, possibly because they were hunted by sailors and their rats and cats!

Who's strange looking?

MARINE IGUANA

The only sea-swimming iguanas on Earth. After a big swim they sneeze out all the salty sea water.

BALTRA →

ACHOOOO!

SANTA CRUZ

SANTA FÉ

SAN CRISTÓBAL

Yellow warbler

ESPAÑOLA

SALLY LIGHTFOOT CRAB

A super-colourful crustacean named after a famous Caribbean dancer.

Let's all look after island life.

Frigate bird

FLOREANA

Woodlands

IF YOU GO DOWN TO THE WOODS TODAY ...

... get ready for an exploring surprise! It won't be just **squirrels**, **rabbits** and **birds** that you see. Woods are homes to big black bears, hungry howling wolves and beak-banging woodpeckers! 30% of the world is covered by woodland which means wonderful woodland creatures can be found all over the planet.

So put on your wellies to explore the woods!

NORTH AMERICA

Pileated woodpecker

Redwoods are among the tallest trees in the world.

Redwood

RED WOLF

Wolves wander around at night and communicate by howling to each other. All dogs are related to the Gray wolf.

Even me!

Robin

EUROPE

Oak

Great tit

Silver birch

SQUIRREL

Squirrels help new trees to grow such as the mighty oak by burying their acorns to eat later on. The ones they forget about turn into trees.

BRILLIANT BUGS

Woodlands are excellent for a bit of bug spotting. How many bugs can you spot?

Ice Worlds

BRR! IT'S COLD OUT THERE!

Are YOU brave enough to explore the *iciest* place on EARTH? These ice-loving animals have evolved over millions of years so they can survive the harshest habitats on the planet - the North and the South Pole. And all good Arctic explorers know to look for the **North Pole** in the Arctic Circle and the **South Pole** in the Antarctic Circle ...

So pull on an extra pair of pants ... it's about to get **ICY!**

ARCTIC FOX

In the winter months this fox's fur is bright white. In summer it turns brown or grey to blend in with the environment.

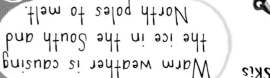

Warm weather is causing the ice in the South and North poles to melt.

So protect our poles!

Nooo!!!

Too late, Ernest!

FAMOUS EXPLORERS

The most famous polar explorer, Sir Ernest Shackleton, attempted to get to the South Pole first but was beaten by Norwegian explorer Roald Amundsen.

Albatross

Dress up as a POLAR EXPLORER

Skis

Warm coat

Scarf

Warm mittens

Ear muffs

Woolly hat

Deserts

SNAKES, SCORPIONS, SPIDERS, LIZARDS!

Exploring deserts probably makes you think of **slithering, sandy creatures** hiding from heat and sunshine, but that's not always the case! The Arctic and Antarctica are also called deserts because they have so little rainfall. WOW! We've already **explored** those icy poles though.

Hang on to your sunhats, things are about to get HOT ...

Dress up as a desert explorer

A good hat

Sunscreen

Sunglasses

Light, cool clothes

Water, water and EVEN MORE water!

Sandals

THE POISONOUS ...

Be careful where you step. You wouldn't want to be bitten by a **Horned viper**. Scientists believe its horns protect its eyes.

Deathstalker scorpions
They are one of the world's most deadliest scorpions.

THE STRANGE ...

The **Thorny devil** lives in central Australia. Named because of its thorny body, which protects it from hungry predators, it drinks water from its feet!

I'm thirsty

Long back legs that are excellent for jumping out of danger.

JERBOAS

These rodents live in the deserts of North-west China and Southern Mongolia. Jerboas have amazing hearing to listen out for predators. Look at those ears!

SAHARA DESERT

Deserts are found all over the world but one of the most famous deserts of all is in North Africa. The Sahara is the largest HOT desert. Temperatures can, on average, reach up to 50°c in the summer. HOT, HOT, HOT!

Hot, hot, hot

ANCIENT EGYPTIANS

Thousands of years ago, when Pharaohs walked the Sahara, it would have looked very different. Heavy rains at the time allowed plants and trees to grow SO large that animals such as giraffes, lions and rhinos lived there.

Two rows of eyelashes help me to flutter away the desert sands.

Camel spiders can eat entire rodents like mice and rats.

Deserts are more than just sand dunes!

Desert rat

THE HEAD IN THE SAND ...
The Red-necked ostrich is the world's largest bird but it can't fly.

CAMELS

Saharan camels (Dromedary camels) have one hump while camels from other parts of the world have two (Bactrian camels). Its hump is made of fat which gives the camel energy when there isn't much food.

Herring gull

Gannet

Wow!

Oceans

Dolphin

SPLASH! What's that lurking beneath the waves?

Oceans cover about 71% of planet Earth and contain some of the most **extraordinary** creatures explorers have **ever** seen. From the strange-looking **Blobfish** to the beautiful **Angelfish**, there is plenty more to find. In fact, we've only fully explored 5% of the oceans so far which means explorers know more about the surface of the Moon!

So take a deep breath and dive right in ...

Among the coral, can you spot ...

Sponges

Crabs

Balloonfish

Clownfish

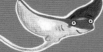
Stingrays

Angelfish

Lionfish

Seahorses

Cod

Blue tang

CORAL REEF
Beautifully coloured reefs are mostly made up of spiky, living organisms called polyps ... OUCH!

There's even a poo-like sea cucumber! WEIRD!

Starfish

I can see in the dark

Parrotfish

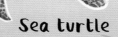
Sea turtle

Moray eel

OCTOPUS

There's no other creature like an octopus on Earth. It's an alien-looking creature with blue blood. Each arm has its own brain.

GREAT WHITE SHARK

They can grow longer than the height of a giraffe.

OCEAN SUNFISH

They are the heaviest known fish on Earth!

I'M OLD

The oldest fish ever discovered is the **Greenland shark**.

DEEP SEA

Down in the deepest layer of the ocean live creatures that GLOW IN THE DARK! Oooooh!

BOX JELLYFISH

They are one of the deadliest animals in the world.

Dumbo octopus

MARIANA TRENCH

The deepest part of the ocean is equal to the height of 34 Eiffel Towers. Only three people have ever made it to the bottom.

In 1960, Jacques Piccard and Don Walsh were the first people to make it to the bottom of the Trench. IF **YOU** make it this far you might bump into the biggest animal in the world ...

The siphonophore

Angler Fish

Nighttime

WHAT'S THAT SNORTING IN THE DARK?

Exploring animals isn't just for daytime. When the stars are out and you're tucked up in bed, it's time for a whole world of different animals to wake up. And these animals love to **spring**, **screech**, **dart** and **dive** just as much as daytime animals do.

So grab your torch and find out what's hiding in the dark ...

LUNA MOTH

Luna moths don't have mouths!

Nope, not hungry

Glow-worms

BADGER

Badgers live in groups in underground burrows called sets.

SMALL-SPOTTED GENET

These cat-like animals have long tails to help them balance when leaping from tree to tree.

Axolotl

Location: Mexico
Habitat: Lakes and canals
Size: Up to 45cm
An AMAZING salamander that can regrow parts of its body such as arms, legs, jaws, brain and spine.

Super-cool animal spotters

Pebble toad

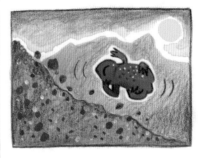

Location: Venezuela
Habitat: Tepui mountains
Size: Up to 3cm
These amphibians can roll up into a ball and bounce away like pebbles.

Strange Creatures

YOU NEVER KNOW WHEN YOU MIGHT DISCOVER SOMETHING NEW ...

So when exploring, keep your eyes wide, your ears open and your super-cool animal spotters on! The world is FULL of incredible creatures in all shapes and sizes. There aren't enough pages in this book to tell you about them all BUT here are a few of the **weirdest**, **wildest**, most **wonderful** creatures on Earth.

Have YOU ever seen a ...

Pink fairy armadillo

Location: Argentina
Habitat: Desert
Size: Up to 16cm
This crazy creature keeps cool by pumping blood into its shell, turning it pink.

Okapi

Location: Central Africa
Habitat: Ituri Rainforest
Size: Up to 2.5m
Okapis are related to giraffes.

Proboscis monkey

Location: Borneo
Habitat: Jungle
Size: Up to 76cm
This monkey has the longest nose of all primates.

Goblin shark

Location: Japanese coast
Habitat: Deep sea
Size: Up to 6m
This snappy species has been around for millions of years.

Shoebill

Location: East Africa
Habitat: Wetlands
Size: Up to 115cm
This bold bird eats baby crocodiles by using its huge bill (beak).

Duck-billed platypus

Location: Australia
Habitat: Rivers
Size: Up to 60cm
Only one of two mammals on Earth that lays eggs!

WOW!

Endangered Animals

ANIMALS NEED YOUR HELP!

Explorers don't just look for **animals**, they protect them too. **Explorers** all around the world are figuring out how to look after animals in danger. They are **helping** to stop animals that are hunted by humans (poachers) or they are learning more about what animals need to survive. Even the **bees** in your back garden need help finding flowers!

> Please don't cut down our trees

SUMATRAN ORANGUTAN
Critically endangered

Location: Sumatra, Indonesia
Population: 13,000 left
Fact: Can eat by using their feet

> Which of these rare animals can you spot in the pages of this book?

SHORT-CRESTED COQUETTE HUMMINGBIRD
Critically endangered

Location: Mexico
Population: Up to 1,000 left
Fact: The smallest birds on Earth

SUNDA TIGER
Critically endangered

Location: Sumatra, Indonesia
Population: Only 400 left
Fact: Unlike most cats, tigers love water

CASSOWARY
Endangered

Location: Australia
Population: 4,600 left
Fact: A direct descendant of DINOSAURS!

Please help us by not catching us in your nets

VAQUITA
Critically endangered

Location: Gulf of California, Mexico
Population: 10 left
Fact: Smallest marine mammal

SAOLA
Critically endangered

Location: Vietnam and Laos
Population: 750 left
Fact: Also known as the Asian unicorn

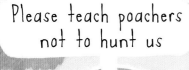

Please teach poachers not to hunt us

BLACK RHINO
Critically endangered

Location: Africa
Population: 5,600 left
Fact: Run on their toes

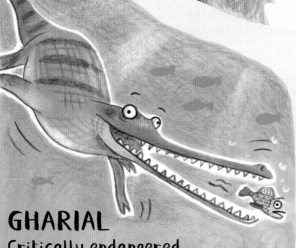

GHARIAL
Critically endangered

Location: India and Nepal
Population: 650 left
Fact: Long nose to help when fishing

You can help too!

HONEY BEE
Endangered

Location: Found worldwide
Population: Unknown
Fact: Queen bees can live up to five years

Also available:

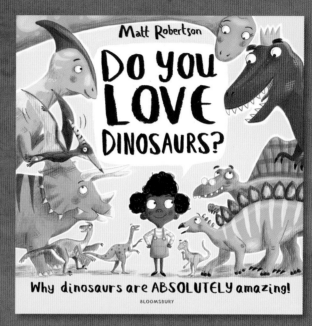

Crawly! Hairy! Maybe a bit **scary?** Bugs are ACTUALLY truly BRILLIANT and there's something new to learn about every single one in **DO YOU LOVE BUGS?** - Winner of a Sainsbury's Children's Book Award 2020.

Stomp, chomp, ROAAAAAR! Some dinosaurs had a deadly bite, others could run fast and some could make the smelliest of farts ... POO-WEE! Dive headfirst into the wonderful world of dinosaurs in **DO YOU LOVE DINOSAURS?**

Find these books at all good bookshops and libraries, or visit www.bloomsbury.com